astonish

astonis

astonish

astonish

astonish

astonish

astonish

astonish

astonish

astonish

astonish

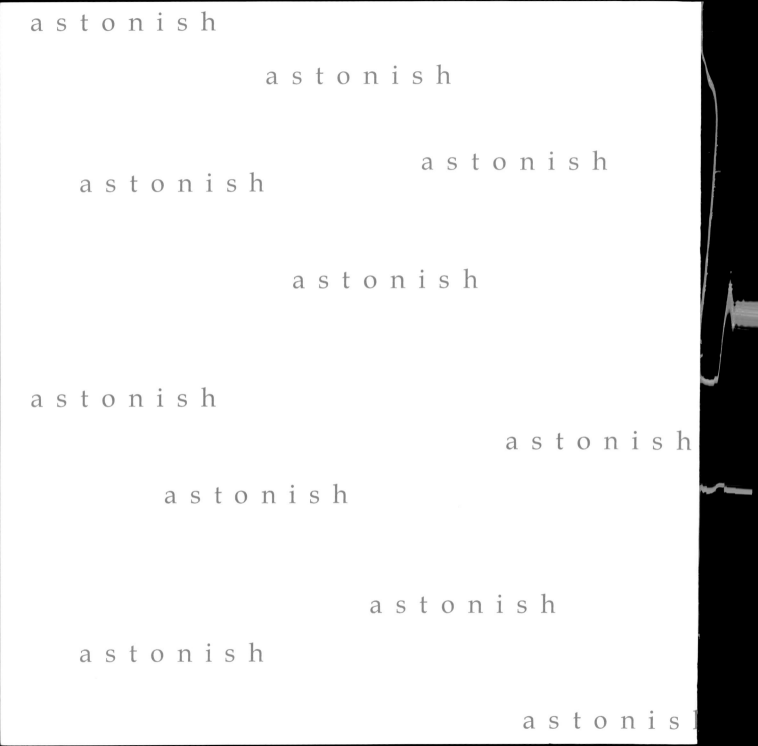

a s t o n i s h

jodi hills

TRISTAN PUBLISHING

MINNEAPOLIS

Dedication

To all the teachers of Washington Elementary, Central Junior High, and Jefferson Senior High. My mother worked in the superintendent's office throughout my schooling years. At home in the evenings, she would still answer our phone, "Alexandria Public Schools." The imprint was strong. The imprint remains. Mrs. Bergstrom taught me how to spell. Mr. Iverson taught me how to write a poem. Mrs. Anderson gave me a locker and a safe place to call mine. I can't name them all, I would need another book. As sure as I still hear my mother's voice, I hear the place that most likely saved us both — Alexandria Public Schools.

Library of Congress Cataloging-in-Publication Data

Names: Hills, Jodi - author, illustrator.
Title: Astonish / written and illustrated by Jodi Hills.
Description: Golden Valley : Tristan Publishing, 2019.
Identifiers: LCCN 2019014797 | ISBN 9781939881212 (alk. paper)
Subjects: LCSH: Surprise. | Creative ability.
Classification: LCC BF575.S8 H55 2019 | DDC 153.3/5--dc23
LC record available at https://lccn.loc.gov/2019014797

TRISTAN Publishing, Inc.
2355 Louisiana Avenue North
Golden Valley, MN 55427

Jodi Hills is an author and artist, originally from Minnesota, now living, loving, and creating in the south of France. The best "bio" of Jodi is in her work. In her books and in her paintings, she offers her heart, soul, and life experience.

www.jodihills.com

Text copyright ©2019, Jodi Hills   ISBN 978-1-939881-21-2   First Printing   Printed in the USA

"With an apple, I will astonish Paris."

Paul Cézanne

Maybe the greatest gift given is the ability to see the gifts at all.

FOR THEY DON'T ALL COME WRAPPED IN
RIBBONS AND BOWS. THEY DON'T ALL
ARRIVE WITH SMILES.

SOME REST IN THE CORNERS, WAITING.
BEHIND THE DAMAGE AND THE DUST.

THEY ARE GIVEN, WILLING, READY,
— IN SIMPLICITY AND SURPRISE —
PREPARED TO ASTONISH.

Where it came from — I don't know. It was just there, the empty frame in my room. Just this one. Golden. Waiting. *Hopeful*. In *my* room. I never questioned it, in the way that one doesn't question a pure gift. It was there, and I knew

I HAD TO FILL IT.

I sat alone in my tiny room. Paper, crayons, and pencils in hand, I began to draw my world, **CREATE MYSELF A LIFE.** I had to. I had to be something. *I was not going to disappear.* For that was the true fear — not the angry words that so often filled the house.

"You're nothing," he said. How could he think so? I was only a child. I colored brightly. I could have believed him. And that could have been my ending. It would have been easy. But there was this frame. And my hands.

I CHOSE NOT TO END, BUT TO *begin!*

THE PAPER CAME TO LIFE. The colors jumped from the paper. No matter how many times he told me I was nothing, the paper said something different. *I had been given a gift.* The gift of an empty frame. The gift to make a choice.

With paper and colors,

I PAINTED HIM WRONG.

I didn't have the words for
it then, at five; but somehow
I knew, with all the certainty
of Cézanne, that

THIS
WAS
MY
APPLE.

When Cézanne said, *"With an apple, I will astonish Paris,"*

some may have found it bold

— and maybe it was —

but sometimes

WE HAVE TO BE.

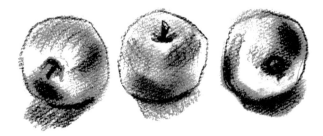

YOU HAVE TO BE BOLD to take the ordinary and make it extraordinary. To take this life and make it astonishing.

And that's what Cézanne did when he painted an apple. With care and thought and heart, he brought the painting to life.

It didn't shout. It didn't shock. It didn't need to. Because it breathed. It was alive!

NOW THAT'S *astonishing.*

He knew that with this simple object — *this simply beautiful apple* — he could change the way you saw things.

He could take something ordinary and make it

EXTRAORDINARY.

 He could hold your **HEART** in the palm of his hands.

TAKE YOUR BREATH AWAY with something you yourself had held, had touched.

It was something so simple, so beautiful, so attainable, that it made you want to reach for it. Believe in it. Hold out your own hands and know that in this life there is real beauty —

**RIGHT THERE IN FRONT OF YOU —
FOR YOU.**

He reached out his hand with a brush

and painted an apple

and told you that it was all possible.

IT IS POSSIBLE.

And breathless, with nothing but hope and desire,

YOU BELIEVE IT.

A gift that makes

believing possible —

MAKES BELIEVING POSSIBLE —

that's bold,
that's beyond beauty,
that's astonishing!

I didn't know that PARIS existed, but I, too, was going to be

bold enough to change the way the world saw things, the way

he saw things, the way I was seen.

I was going to be **BOLD ENOUGH. BRAVE ENOUGH.**

I was going to be **ENOUGH**, just me, just my tear-stained,

color-filled hands, I was going to be enough to fill that empty frame.

AND THAT HAD TO BE SOMETHING!

I had never heard of Cézanne.

I had not even read a book on art.

But that magic was in the air, the universe.

THAT MAGIC REMAINS IN THE AIR.

For all of us.

This power to astonish lives in us, and all around us. This power to astonish, to make us change the way we are seen, to change the way the world is seen — it's right here. It sits on our tables and in our hearts.

A GIFT JUST WAITING TO BE OPENED.

A FRAME JUST WAITING TO BE FILLED.

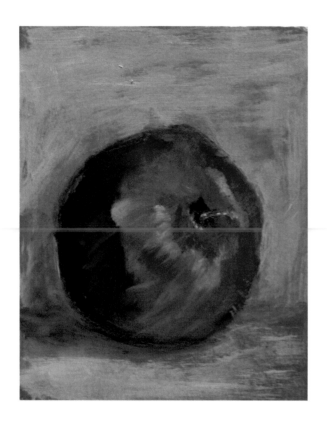

BUT IT NEEDS YOU.

There's a gift that's just for you, but you have to claim it.

YOU HAVE TO DARE TO SAY, *That's mine.*

YOU HAVE TO DARE to give of yourself, as freely as the gift was given. As freely as this gift said **YES** to you, you have to do the same. You have to say, yes, I see!

You have to be bold enough to embrace it, even when others will tell you it isn't there. That YOU aren't there. You have to be bold enough to say, I have been given a gift. I have been given a life that is worthy of being seen. I am here. And that is something!

I am really something.

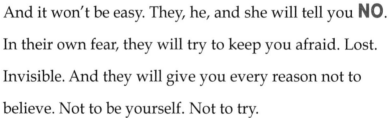

And it won't be easy. They, he, and she will tell you **NO**. In their own fear, they will try to keep you afraid. Lost. Invisible. And they will give you every reason not to believe. Not to be yourself. Not to try.

But it is in you. **YOUR APPLE.**

That thing that coddles your soul,

colors your life,

lifts your heart, challenges your mind,

makes you human,

MAKES YOU — YOU!

That's your apple.

Your apple. The thing that **YOU ARE WILLING TO DO AGAIN AND AGAIN.** The thing you wake up early for. Stay up all night for.

The thing that makes the red bleed through your every muscle and **MAKES YOU FEEL MORE ALIVE** than you ever have.

THE APPLE THAT SPEAKS LOUDER THAN ANY NEGATIVE VOICE AROUND YOU.

The apple that says YES. The apple that keeps you alive, keeps you trying, shows you the beauty of the struggle and the victory.

Just by filling your frame,

living your true life,

using your true gift,

YOU WILL BE ASTONISHING.

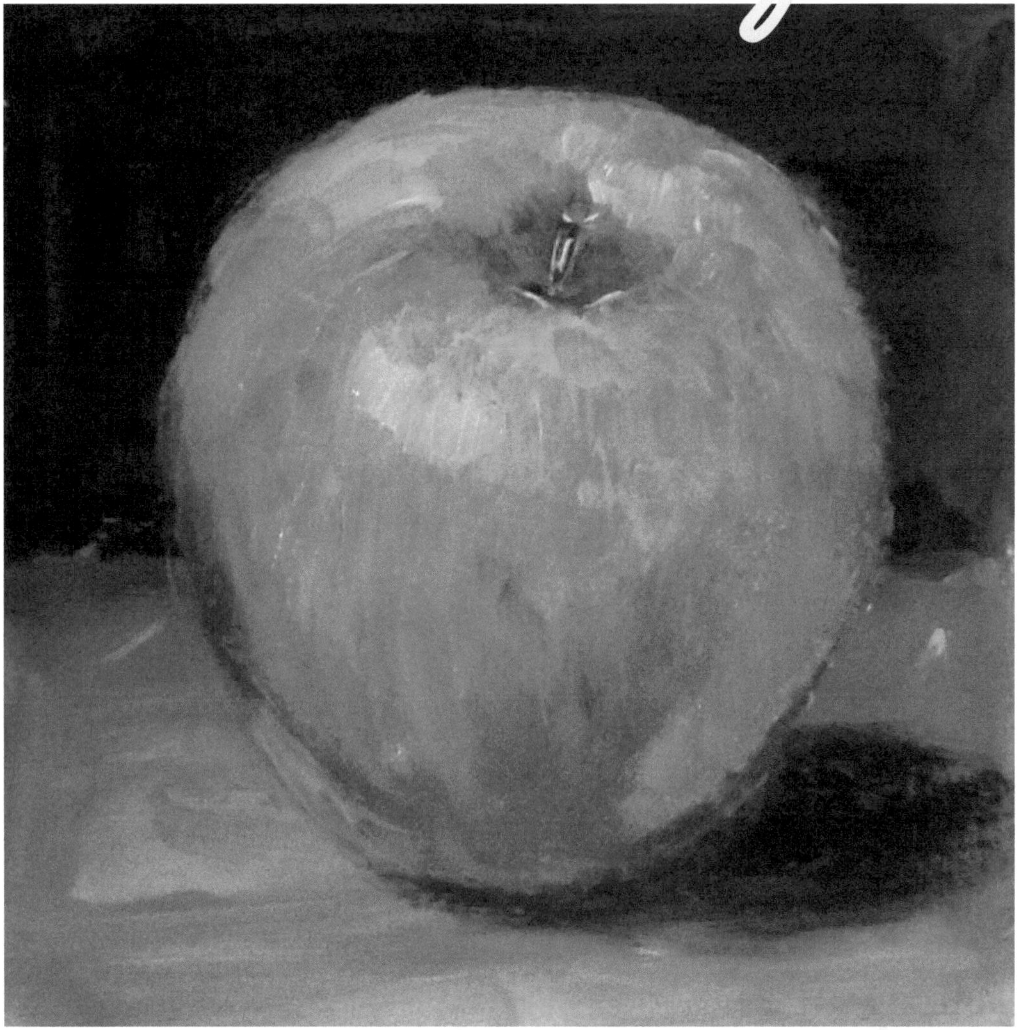

THE TRULY ASTONISHING THING is that there is a world of people doing the same. This is who you surround yourself with — people using their gifts every day to make this world beautiful. To make this world **BIGGER THAN PARIS.**
BIGGER THAN NEW YORK. Bigger and more beautiful than any of us have ever seen.

A world of people opening doors and highways and hearts, just by living. Just by being bold enough to be themselves and to share their amazing gifts, they, too, give us reasons every day, to hope, to believe, to try.

FIND THEM. SEE THEM.

LISTEN TO THEM.

EVERY TIME someone dances, that dance stomps on the words, "No, you can't."

Every time someone tells their story, that story erases the words, "You're not special."

EVERY TIME SOMEONE PAINTS, THAT PAINTING COVERS THE WORDS, "YOU'RE NOTHING."

Someone is doing that for you.
You can do it too!

Maybe you were born to paint. To dance. To write. To create.

It's your thing — it's your apple — **YOU KNOW WHAT IT IS.**

Maybe you were put here to solve problems.

To discover. Nurture. Build. Invent.

You know it in your heart.

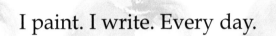

I paint. I write. Every day.

Look around.

Right now **SOMEONE IS DARING** to get on that stage.

Someone is going to class. Crossing lines and putting out fires.

Someone is planting. Molding. Reforming. Changing laws.

Someone is breaking stereotypes and knocking down barriers.

Right now someone is raising children.

Right now, you are thinking, **MAYBE I CAN . . .**

Right now, **YOU ARE WILLING TO TRY.**

Right now, the world is welcoming your apple.

YOUR BEAUTIFUL, GLORIOUS,

ASTONISHING APPLE.

Right now, I tell you that I made it out of my tiny bedroom. I made
it to New York. I made it to Paris. I have walked the steps of Cézanne
in Provence. But more importantly, I have walked the steps of my
own heart.

I HAVE PAINTED MYSELF TO LIFE.
I HAVE WRITTEN MY OWN STORY.

With my apple, I have filled my frame. With my apple,
I have astonished myself.

Right now, I'm looking at you. The Eiffel Tower fades.
Reds and golds and greens shine in your eyes so brightly,
and the world is ready to be astonished by you.

ISN'T THAT SOMETHING?!!!

———————◆———————

DO YOUR THING — *whatever that may be* —

THAT THING THAT CODDLES YOUR SOUL —

LIFTS YOUR HEART — CHALLENGES YOUR MIND —

MAKES YOU HUMAN —

MAKES YOU — *you!*

DO THAT — DO THAT EVERY DAY.

That's your apple.

———————◆———————

astonish

The
WORK
BOOK

Creating the daily practices of your astonishing life

AUTHENTIC

Original

ASTONISHING

*"I began to draw my world.
Create myself a life. I had to."*

There are no rules to say that we have to enjoy our lives. No regulations that say we have to accomplish our goals. No patrols to say that we have to act like it matters, that it all matters. But then there's the heart. The heart that says, "But I have to . . . I have to be . . ." If you're here, reading this, you already understand. You feel it deep down inside you. You have to (you're whispering it to yourself right now.) You are not afraid to believe that there is something pretty spectacular out there, and you want to be a part of it. You need it.

This workbook is meant to help you raise that little voice inside of you. To tell it, "You are not alone." To tell it, "Yes, you can." To tell it, "You are really something, someone!"

Let's start right now. Write down your name, your astonishing gift. Name it. Claim it!

ASTONISH!

There's a gift that's just for you, but you have to claim it.

YOU HAVE TO DARE TO SAY,

"THAT'S MINE."

My name is _____

My astonishing gift is _____

_____

_____

In my studio. Aix en Provence.

I HAVE PAINTED MYSELF TO LIFE.

Now I live in the land of Cézanne. People may say, "Oh, well, you're inspired because you live there." And yes, it is a very inspiring landscape, and I feel lucky.

But I must tell you, I was inspired every day, for years, when the only place I had to paint was in my bathroom. I lived in a tiny apartment. I would sit on the closed toilet seat, balance the canvas on one knee and the bathtub, and I could paint for hours.

Inspiration can be everywhere,

MY INSPIRATION

_____

_____

_____

_____

_____

_____

_____

_____

_____

_____

_____

_____

_____

 # TIME

The easiest thing to say is, "I don't have time for that." The truth is — we all have time. We have time every day. And every day we get more time. Another day, filled with time. The question is, what are you going to do with it? I know you're busy. We're all busy. We all have things and people and places to fill our days. So what are you going to do? What's the best choice for you?

THE HOUR I CAN'T LIVE WITHOUT — EVERY DAY!

_____

_____

_____

_____

_____

MY PERFECT DAY INCLUDES:

_____

_____

_____

_____

_____

_____

_____

My Time

_____

_____

_____

_____

_____

_____

_____

_____

_____

_____

GOOD MORNING, SUNSHINE!

I like brioche for breakfast. Brioche takes a day to make. Do I have time for that? Yes. Because I like it. I like the scent in the kitchen. I like that my hands make something that wasn't there the day before. I like when my husband says, "Ça sent bon!" I like sitting across the table from him, enjoying something I made. Slowly. Starting my day with this pleasure is immeasurable. Or, if you must measure it, let's say it's huge. C'est grand! I have the time to feel good. You have that time too. Maybe you're not a morning person. We're all different. But we can all begin our day, no matter what hour that is, with something positive.

THIS IS MY "BRIOCHE!"

_____

_____

_____

_____

_____

"... it won't be easy. They, he, and she will tell you, **NO**.
In their own fear, they will try to keep you afraid. Lost. Invisible. And they will give you every reason not to believe. Not to be yourself. Not to try.

But it is in you.

YOUR APPLE."

Today, take the "if" out of your vocabulary and just do it. Listen only to the voice that says, "Yes, you can!"

YOU ARE NOT LOST.
YOU ARE NOT INVISIBLE.

~~IF~~ I COULD DO ANYTHING . . .

Getting rid of the *if*s! Make a list of what you can do!

FINDING BEAUTY

For me, it's always been about the little things. Maybe it's gratitude. Maybe it's grace. Maybe it's having a good mother who pointed out those things. Take a look around. It's an amazing world.

 TAKE A LOOK IN THE MIRROR — YOU'RE PRETTY AMAZING TOO!

You don't need money to find beautiful things.

OPEN YOUR DOORS. OPEN YOUR WINDOWS. NATURE IS FOR ALL OF US. THOSE RAINDROPS ON THE FLOWER PETALS. FOR YOU! THAT SUNSET. YOURS. THAT OPEN PATH —THAT'S RIGHT, IT'S OPEN FOR YOU! BEAUTIFUL!

HOLD OUT YOUR OWN HANDS AND KNOW THAT IN THIS LIFE, THERE IS REAL BEAUTY.

I AM NOT A PROFESSIONAL PHOTOGRAPHER, BUT I DO LOVE TAKING PICTURES. THE LENS OFFERS A NEW VIEW. WHEN I AM PAINTING, SOMETIMES I STOP AND TAKE A PICTURE OF MY WORK, AND LOOK AT IT THROUGH THIS DIFFERENT EYE. THERE IS SO MUCH TO SEE WHEN I LOOK AT IT FROM A DIFFERENT PERSPECTIVE. IF YOU ARE STUCK IN YOUR PROJECT, TAKE OUT YOUR PHONE, TAKE OUT YOUR CAMERA, AND LOOK AT IT WITH A NEW LENS. THIS PHOTO OPPORTUNITY JUST MIGHT TURN INTO A REAL OPPORTUNITY.

READING lifts up your brain to all kinds of new levels.
Write down the books that elevate your senses.

- _____
- _____
- _____
- _____
- _____
- _____

Find a podcast on your favorite subject. They have everything. Listen to people doing, trying, creating, and succeeding.

Surround yourself with people who try. These people will always make a difference, and so will you!

MUSIC stirs your soul. List the songs that raise you out of your seat.

- _____
- _____
- _____
- _____
- _____
- _____

WHETHER
YOU'RE AN
ARTIST OR AN
ENGINEER, IT
NEVER HURTS
TO TAKE A
MINUTE AND
JUST COLOR.

INSIDE THE
LINES. OR
 OUTSIDE. IT'S
ALL UP TO YOU.
COLOR YOUR
PAGE. COLOR
YOUR LIFE.
COLOR YOUR
WORLD.

OUT ON A LIMB

YOU'RE GOING TO HAVE TO TAKE RISKS. BE UNCERTAIN. VULNERABLE. THERE'S THE MAGIC.

When you're open, asking questions, exposed, trying something new, anything can happen. Make it fun. Get yourself used to change. Take 30 days and make sure you do something new every day. They can be small changes or big chances. Your choice.

EAT SOMETHING NEW. MEET SOMEONE. TAKE A DIFFERENT ROUTE TO SCHOOL. SEND OFF YOUR MANUSCRIPT. SEND THAT EMAIL. CLIMB A MOUNTAIN. SHOW YOUR PAINTINGS. DANCE ON THE SUBWAY. RAISE YOUR HAND. ASK THE QUESTION. TELL YOURSELF WHAT YOU REALLY WANT. TELL YOURSELF WHO YOU REALLY WANT TO BE. THEN, MORE THAN ANYTHING ELSE, FIND YOURSELF THE LONGEST LIMB, AND **DARE TO BE THAT PERSON!**

30 NEW THINGS
ABOUT ME

You have to get through those little struggle patches on the way to magic. And you can. Commit yourself to the work.

IT TAKES A FEW STROKES

You have to put in the time. Work at it. Don't get discouraged. There's always a brief moment in a painting when I wonder — "Is this really it? Do I go on? This doesn't look like it . . . wait . . . maybe . . ." and then I plow through. And I reach the magic point where I know this is going to work, and then I work longer.

THERE ARE TIMES WHEN MY SOUL SAYS,

"FORGET EVERYTHING — today you are a gardener. GRAB HOLD THIS SHOVEL, AND DIG DEEP."

My commitment to my apple.
My commitment to myself.

_____

_____

_____

_____

_____

_____

_____

_____

_____

Your apple. The thing that **YOU ARE WILLING TO DO AGAIN AND AGAIN.**

The thing you wake up early for. Stay up all night for.

WHERE IS YOUR PARIS?

The world is a pretty big place. A pretty wonderful place. The more you see, the more you will want to see. If you have the means to travel by plane, by car, by boat — do it! If you have enough for train fare, hop on. A bus, a bicycle, your own feet can always get you somewhere. If you can't physically leave, read, read, and read some more. Libraries are still free. Books are passports. Meet people who don't look like you. Let them teach you. Let them take you places with just a conversation. There is no limit to how you can travel.

Cézanne wanted to astonish Paris. Where is your Paris? My first "Paris" was Minneapolis. My second, Chicago. Then New York. Then really Paris! Set your goals and reach them. Set some more. Go farther.

THE WORLD IS WAITING FOR YOU!

PLACES I WANT TO SEE

_____

_____

_____

_____

_____

PLACES I WANT TO BE SEEN

_____

_____

_____

_____

_____

BE CURIOUS

See things from a different angle. A new perspective. If you are curious, you will always find a new path, a new way. You will be able to solve problems. Find joy in the most unlikely places. Be empathetic. Find wonder. Curiosity will fill your palette, your mind, and your heart.

TAKE A DAY OFF AND FORGET THE PLANNER. THROW AWAY THE RULE BOOK. TURN OFF THE GPS. OPEN THE DOOR AND SEE WHAT HAPPENS. YOUR FEET WILL TAKE YOU WHERE YOU NEED TO GO.

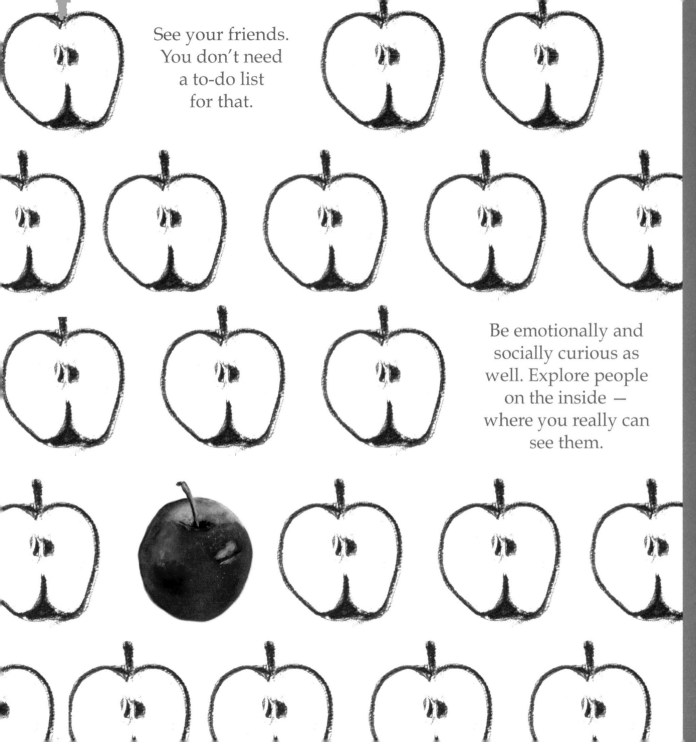

See your friends.
You don't need
a to-do list
for that.

Be emotionally and
socially curious as
well. Explore people
on the inside —
where you really can
see them.

GRATITUDE

No lines. No boundaries on these pages. Just as gratitude should be. Take the time to write it down. In any format. Then let it roll off the pages.

TASTE

Life is a lot like cooking. You can follow a recipe, but ultimately, it comes down to taste.

And how do you develop your taste? You have to try a few things. See what you like. I can hear my mother saying, "How do you know you don't like it, if you don't try it?" Who knew this could apply to almost anything? Try it. If you don't like it, change it. If you like it, make some more.

And whatever you do, do it well. Imagine you are putting your own guarantee on everything you touch. Let the world know, *I made this, I did this,* and be proud of it. Show the world your unique abilities, your original taste. Show the world **YOU**!

FILL YOUR HEART.
FEED YOUR SOUL.
TASTE THIS LIFE.

THERE ARE SO MANY THINGS THAT ARE UNIQUE ABOUT YOU.

You have been given these gifts for a reason. Be generous with your gifts.
You can't share them unless you acknowledge what they are. Write them
down. *Don't forget to smile. You already are!*

_____

_____

_____

_____

_____

_____

_____

_____

_____

YOU KNOW WHAT IT IS

Your core holds the voice that speaks louder than any negative voice around you.

KEEPING YOUR CORE

(DOESN'T MEAN YOU CAN'T CHANGE YOUR MIND.)

What's at your core — this must never change. What you believe with all your heart — the truth that makes you you — it's what holds you together. Knowing what's deep inside of you — with certainty and conviction — this will make you happier on your happiest of days, and stronger on your toughest. Knowing this, be assured there will be a million daily things thrown at you. Things to trip you up, change your direction, and even change your mind. And don't be afraid of this. Change is not always easy, but sometimes it's the best thing that can happen. On the days when you're stuck, give your mind a rest. Give it a new perspective. Go for a walk. Listen to music. Take a swim. Eat a cupcake. Ride your bike. Change your clothes. Do something to separate yourself, and then take a fresh look. You may be thrust into a whole new direction. Hold on to your core and enjoy the ride!

Things to do WHEN I'M STUCK

Make yourself a list of your favorite distractions. When you have this at hand, you don't have to think about it — just do it. Your mind will thank you.

_____

_____

_____

_____

_____

_____

_____

YOU KNOW BEST *(for you)*

Once you know your vision, your core, your strengths, your special gift — your apple — the only thing left to do is live it. Success can come in every degree, but remember, the work itself — whatever it is: the writing, the painting, the dancing, the living of your uniquely gifted being — can give you everything.

You know best for you. You know what will fulfill you. You set the bar for yourself. Others' successes do not hurt you. Be happy for them. Others' failures do not lift you. They may not even feel they've failed. They get to decide that for themselves.

Find joy in the doing. The being. You decide who you are. And the definition is decided by you. A writer writes. A painter paints. You are not defined by awards or titles. You are defined by you. Enjoy that.

Have some fun. Think of the best birthday present you ever received. Maybe it was your first bicycle. The first time you rode it up and down the street where you lived. The freedom. The wind in your hair. How glorious it felt. Living out your true gift, multiply that feeling by a million, and again! It's a joy to be you! Allow yourself that! LET'S RIDE!!!!

THIS IS NO ENDING. THIS IS WHERE YOU BEGIN. WRITE YOURSELF A LETTER. BE YOUR OWN EXPERT. YOUR OWN ADVOCATE. CHEERLEADER. FRIEND. CONFIDANTE. TELL YOURSELF WHAT YOU NEED TO HEAR. WHEN IN DOUBT, KEEP IT SIMPLE. KEEP IT HONEST. KEEP IT KIND.

Dear _____ ,

_____

_____

_____

_____

_____

_____

_____

_____

_____

All my best,

# OH, I ALMOST FORGOT . . .

Some of your best ideas will come when you're not even trying. When you lie down to sleep. In the shower. Always keep a pen nearby. I've used lipliner, crayons, whatever is closest; but a pen, a pencil, now that can make life grand. I used to think, "If it's important, I'll remember it." . . . umm . . . write it down. You'll thank me later. You can label these pages whatever you like. Notes from the shower. Notes from my pillow. Wherever lightning strikes you, be prepared to write it down.

ABOVE ALL

Always be true to yourself. Be yourself. Sounds so simple. Sounds so hard. Always true. You know your heart. You know your mind. Now use them. You know you are enough. Just you. You are enough to astonish this world.

You don't have to blend TO BELONG.

With my apple,
I have astonished myself.

ISN'T THAT SOMETHING?!!!